OTHER HELEN EXLEY GIFTBOOKS:

To my Daughter with Love
Daughters...
In Celebration of Women
An Illustrated Girl's Notebook
To a very special Son
A Special Collection in Praise of Mothers
An Illustrated Mother's Notebook
An Illustrated Grandmother's Notebook

Published simultaneously in 1997 by Exley Publications Ltd in Great Britain and
Exley Publications LLC in the USA.

12 11 10 9 8 7 6 5 4 3 2 1

Selection and arrangement copyright © Helen Exley 1997.
The moral right of the author has been asserted.

ISBN 1-85015-964-5

Words and pictures selected by Helen Exley.
With special thanks to Margaret Montgomery for her help with text research.
Border illustrations by Angela Kerr.
Pictures researched by Image Select International.
Typeset by Delta, Watford.
Printed in UAE.

Exley Publications Ltd, 16 Chalk Hill, Watford, Herts WD1 4BN, UK.
Exley Publications LLC, 232 Madison Avenue, Suite 1206, NY 10016, USA.

In Praise and Celebration of

DAUGHTERS

A HELEN EXLEY GIFTBOOK

⧣EXLEY
NEW YORK • WATFORD, UK

She is yours to hold in your cupped hands,

to guard and to guide. Give her your strength and

wisdom and all the good that life can offer.

Yours is a sacred trust. Never harm her with

words that can bite and sting. Lead her into truth.

MICHELE GUINNESS, FROM *"TAPESTRY OF VOICES"*

When you are a father, and you hear your children's voices, you will feel that those little ones are akin to every drop in your veins; that they are the very flower of your life and you will cleave so closely to them that you seem to feel every movement that they make.

HONORE DE BALZAC (1799-1850),
FROM *"LE PERE GORIOT"*

Nothing I've ever done has given me more joys and rewards than being a father to my children.

BILL COSBY

A small child sits and spreads her arms.
"Mummay. Dadday. Nannay. Diz-wiz. Pop.
Me."
And in that gesture gathers us to her heart.
Her people.
Her loves.
Her world.

PAM BROWN, b.1928

*The whisper of a baby girl
can be heard further than the
roar of a lion.*

ARAB PROVERB

*A tiny daughter gives parents
a life in a climate of
perpetual wonder.*

PIERRE DOUCET

Her open mouth groping on my cheek gives me I can't say what pleasure, it is almost a pain of happiness to feel her oneness with me, her absolute dependance on me, and her knowledge that it is well for her that she has me.

HELEN THOMAS,
IN A LETTER TO HER HUSBAND,
FROM *"UNDER STORM'S WING"*

In the evening, after she has gone to sleep, I kneel beside the crib and touch her face, where it is pressed against the slats, with mine.

JOAN DIDION

What feeling is so nice as a child's hand in yours? So small, so soft and warm, like a kitten huddling in the shelter of your clasp.

MARJORIE HOLMES

I wonder if you remember
how we loved long days in the
country? How you laughed
when we swung you in the
air? How we all put on our
bright gloves and went
crunching into the snow?
Your little knitted bobble hat?
Your tiny boots? I remember.
I always will.

HELEN THOMSON, b.1943

There is something infinitely precious about having a daughter. Mine, from the moment she was born, drew from me reserves of tenderness, protectiveness and fight I never knew I possessed. I wanted to change the world overnight, to make it a safer, easier, better place for this miniature woman, this receptacle of all my dreams and aspirations, this extension of myself.

MICHELE GUINNESS, FROM *"TAPESTRY OF VOICES"*

All right, I admit it – I was looking forward to a little peace and quiet, when I suggested you might like to go off and have fun with your friends. "But they reckon it's more fun here with you – and I do too," you claimed. What a compliment – and what mother needs peace and quiet anyway, this side of her ninetieth birthday?

CHRISTINE HARRIS, b.1940

What a lot of fuss we make over disappointments and failures and the loss of material things. When all that really matters is that the family have each other – and you.

PAM BROWN, b.1928

My youngest daughter, like my eldest
daughter, like any loved and wanted child, was,
is, worth anything and everything, is
more precious than rubies. There is no way you
can make up a balance sheet, weigh this
against that on some scale.

SUSAN HILL, b.1942, FROM *"FAMILY"*

Dear Daughter. Take my love with you now and into the time that I will never know. It is as much a part of you as breath. Or your identity.

CHARLOTTE GRAY

I wish you all good things – especially the gift of being able to let go. Learn from sorrow and mistakes. Then go on. And most of all I wish you courage. That usually takes care of everything else.

PAM BROWN, b.1928

A new father quickly learns that his child comes to the bathroom at the wrong times. The only way for this father to be certain of bathroom privacy is to shave at the gas station.

BILL COSBY, b.1937

Parents were invented to make children happy by giving them something to ignore.

OGDEN NASH (1902-1971),
RECALLED ON HIS DEATH
MAY 19, 1971

One word of command from me is obeyed by millions... but I cannot get my three daughters, Pamela, Felicity and Joan, to come down to breakfast on time.

VISCOUNT ARCHIBALD WAVELL
(1883-1950)

Every small daughter is an actress to rival Bernhardt.

PAM BROWN, b.1928

Yes, she is a nerve-wracking nuisance, just a noisy bundle of mischief. But when your dreams tumble down and the world is a mess – when it seems you are pretty much of a fool after all – she can make you a king when she climbs on your knee and whispers, "I love you best of all!"

ALAN BECK

My dear daughter, be very good. Do not bump yourself. Do not eat matches. Do not play with scissors or cats. Do not forget your dad. Sleep when your mother wishes it. Love us both. Try to know how we love you. That you will never learn. Goodnight and God keep you, and bless you.
Your Dad.

LETTER BY RICHARD HARDING DAVIS

"Thank heavens for little girls." And they are not just their potential as women. With pigtails and pony tails, in jeans and party dresses, climbing trees, reading books, sucking gobstoppers and turning cartwheels, making friends and breaking friends, they bring their special charm into the world, a delight in detail, a tenderness in relationship, a sensitivity to joy and sorrow and spiritual truth; the many attributes which make them different from little boys.

MICHELE GUINNESS, FROM *"TAPESTRY OF VOICES"*

So, what did I want for this imperious little scrap? Apart from health and perfect happiness, you mean? Nothing. Here's why. When you adore someone utterly, you don't want, you've got. Whatever she is, does, feels is exactly what I like best. When she was the only one in her class who couldn't skip, I was convinced skipping was the most vulgar, ungainly, undesirable activity known to humankind. Only when she got the hang of it, did I realise skipping could be a blast. When she wouldn't sleep, I knew she was far too intelligent to waste a second on slumber. Then, when she finally succumbed to infinitesimal snores, I was soulmates with Sleeping Beauty. She's the sole thing in my life I'm completely satisfied with. The only thing I haven't wanted to swap for something in blue with smaller buttons.

VANESSA FELTZ, FROM "*SHE*" MAGAZINE, MARCH 1997

Having children is like planting seeds
from an unmarked packet.
You vaguely believe that you are going
to get daisies.
Instead, you get orchids,
roses, morning glories, sunflowers....
But all beautiful.
Like you.

PAM BROWN, b.1928

Daughters go through stages – of avoiding washing, of washing obsessively, of ignoring school work, of revising until the early hours, of being anti-everything, of considering entering an enclosed Order. And so on....

They gnaw at your life.

Until one day you break your arm or get pneumonia – and suddenly this aggravating female child is feeding the chooks, exercising the dogs, manning the till, handling phone calls, cooking supper and getting up to siblings crying in the night.

Of course – you get well.

And with a sigh of relief she goes back to being abysmal.

Thank heavens for daughters.

PAM BROWN, b.1928

When our phone rings, it's always for my daughter. When it isn't ringing, it's because she's talking on it. Sometimes when she's on our phone, the neighbors will come over and tell her she's wanted on their phone.

When she leaves, the phone is still a major part of her life. She gives me instructions like this: "Carol is mad at Butch, and Forrest isn't speaking to Jim, so don't mention this to anyone if they call." There's the added comment that I'm to tell Blink to go to Carol's and meet her there. "If Michael calls, tell him I'm at Becky's, so he'll go over there. If Becky calls, don't tell her he's coming, 'cause she would have to tell Jim to go home so Michael wouldn't know he was there. Tell Tom to go to Carol's, and please don't tell him where Blink is."

I made her write it down. After she left, I looked over the instructions and spent the next half hour nervously watching a ball game and living in mortal fear that the phone would ring.

Finally the phone rang. I sprang out of my chair and scanned the instructions one more time. The kid on the phone was Otto. There was no Otto on my list. I took a wild guess and told him to go to Becky's house. He asked me who Becky was.

I hung up. I hate a smart-aleck kid who can't follow simple instructions.

ART FRANK, FROM "*THE SAN FRANCISCO CHRONICLE*", MAY 3, 1987

The house is terribly quiet now, with Arthur in Coronado and you away, and even Lillian admitted that she would be glad to clear up the mess you make when you get through with a fudge orgy, if you were only home.

GROUCHO MARX (1895-1977),
FROM A LETTER TO HIS DAUGHTER, MIRIAM,
IN "LOVE, GROUCHO"

In the dark hours before dawn, I put on the lamp and read your last letter, full of news, full of plans and adventures, opinions and excitements. And the past falls into perspective.

PAM BROWN, b.1928

A Child of Happiness always seems like an old soul living in a new body, and her face is very serious until she smiles, and then the sun lights up the world.... Children of Happiness always look not quite the same as other children. They have strong, straight legs and walk with purpose. They laugh as do all children, and they play as do all children, they talk child talk as do all children, but they are different, they are blessed, they are special, they are sacred.

ANNE CAMERON, FROM *"DAUGHTERS OF COPPER WOMAN"*

How to eat like a child

Spinach:

1. Divide into little piles. Rearrange again into new piles.

2. After five or six maneuvers, sit back and say you are full.

Ice-cream cone:

1. Ask for a double scoop. Knock the top scoop off while walking out of the door of the ice-cream parlor. Cry.

2. Lick the remaining scoop slowly so that the ice cream melts down the outside of the cone and over your hand. Stop licking when the ice cream is even with the top of the cone. Be sure it is absolutely even.

3. Eat a hole in the bottom of the cone and suck the rest of the ice cream out of the bottom.

4. When only the cone remains with ice cream coating the inside, leave on car dashboard.

Chocolate-chip cookies:

1. Half-sit, half-lie on the bed, propped up by a pillow. Read a book. Place cookies next to you on the sheet so that you get crumbs in the bed.

2. As you eat the cookies, remove each chocolate chip and place it on your stomach.

3. When all the cookies are consumed, eat the chips one by one, allowing two per page.

DELIA EPHRON

*She is inventive, original
and takes what she wants from life —
including many of her mother's
clothes. When she comes into a room
she expects something to
happen and, if it doesn't,
she takes steps to see that it does.*

RACHEL BILLINGTON,
FROM *"THE GREAT UMBILICAL"*

With a daughter, life can never, never, never be monotonous.

PAM BROWN, b.1928

Daughters, it should be noted, are prone to moods. The ancient Greek who wrote of Medusa the Gorgon, and her ability to turn men to stone simply by looking at them, had probably just escaped from a confrontation with his daughter.

CHRISTINE HARRIS, b.1940

I have found the best way to give advice to your children is to find out what they want and then advise them to do it.

HARRY S. TRUMAN (1884-1972)

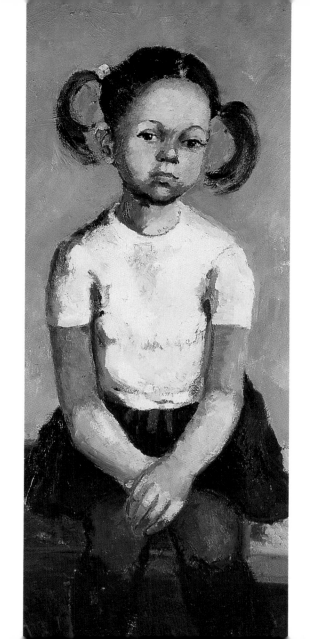

... she is a wise, giving,

deeply loving daughter and friend.

The chasm that existed between us

is now, thankfully, a meadowland

of conversation and love.

DEBBIE REYNOLDS, b.1932, FROM *"DEBBIE: MY LIFE"*

"Darling, do hurry up and change."

"What d'you mean? I *am* changed."

The dialogue between mother and child happens often in the New Year party season when there are occasions that, at least in the parental view, require a certain formality of dress. The "darling, do hurry up," was a response to the sight of a daughter (though the sex is immaterial) dressed in jeans, baggy shirt, short jacket and trainers. "What d'you mean?" was a disingenuous reply since the child knows her mother's meaning very well.

One generation's formal is another generation's anathema. There is, at root, a misunderstanding. If the mother had looked more closely at the child, she would have noticed various points of appearance which indicated a change upwards from the everyday. For example, the hair, although seeming wild and unbrushed to the undiscriminating eye, had just been carefully washed and conditioned. The shirt, though baggy, was also clean and had been ironed (an enormous concession) round the collar. The jacket, embroidered on the back, had been borrowed for the occasion and represented a major fashion decision. The jeans, not blue but black, said at once to anyone who knew anything that this was dressing up for the evening. In the same way, the trainers, being of darkish hue with matching laces, were heading in the direction of conservatism.

All in all, this outfit represented a great deal of thought, time and effort, and it was no wonder that its creator met the "hurry up and change" line with a snarl.

RACHEL BILLINGTON, FROM *"THE FAMILY YEAR"*

Our daughters grow into assured and capable
young women, moving in a world we scarcely know.
It seems at times impossible that they
could have ever been our babies, our toddlers, stomping
after butterflies. Our skinny schoolgirls frisking
along beside us. That these strong hands once clung to ours.
That these confident eyes once sought our reassurance.
Until a day when even the strongest
and the wisest find they need to touch the past
– and they reach out to us.
And we find all they have ever been
is not lost... or ever will be.

PAM BROWN, b.1928

I recall a time in my life during which I was in severe emotional pain. One morning I woke up to find my thirteen-year-old daughter sleeping on the floor beside my bed. When I questioned her about this she quietly told me that she wanted to be near me because she knew I was hurting, but she didn't want to risk disturbing my sleep. The memory of this thoughtful expression of her love and concern still brings tears of gratitude eighteen years later.

BARBARA THOMAS

Violet Elizabeth dried her tears.

She saw that they were useless and she did not

believe in wasting her effects. "All right,"

she said calmly, "I'll thcream then, I'll thcream,

an' thcream, an'thcream till I'm thick."

RICHMAL CROMPTON (1890-1969), FROM *"JUST WILLIAM"*

You must be free to take a path
Whose end I feel no need to know,

...

So you can go without regret
Away from this familiar land,
Leaving your kiss upon my hair
And all the future in your hands.

MARGARET MEAD (1901-1978),
FOR HER DAUGHTER CATHY,
FROM *"BLACKBERRY WINTER"*

Take a sixteen-year-old for a walk
in the country and she can still bound
like the lambs in
the field. Take her to the
seaside and she will still chase the waves
in and out up to her waist. She still likes
snowballing, climbing
up hay bales, rolling down
grassy slopes, lying on the lawn and
watching the clouds turn into
fierce animals.

RACHEL BILLINGTON,
FROM *"THE GREAT UMBILICAL"*

... a man's life will stay like a desert – empty except
for sand – until God endows him with a
daughter such as my little princess. And I also say,
dear lady, that he who does not have a daughter should
adopt one, because the secret and meaning
of time are hidden in the hearts of young girls.

KAHLIL GIBRAN (1883-1931), FROM *"GIBRAN LOVE LETTERS"*

I could look at my daughter and
see the very image I would like to
have been able to hold of myself:
pretty, smart, and with a certain
wisdom beyond her years. I could
discuss my ideas with her and she
would be admiring. I could consult
with her about problems I was
having with "the kids" (her only
slightly younger brother and sister)
and she would be supportive. It was
not as if I was without a partner in
life; I'd lived with Lowell for some
time. Nevertheless, it was my
daughter who often seemed most
meaningful in my struggle for my
lost Self. She was my little Echo, my
"mirror," the answer to a mother's
dreams.

COLETTE DOWLING,
FROM *"PERFECT WOMEN"*

I didn't need to seek out love, I got more than my share of that from my daughter. She and I were a solid unit, and I had a lot to learn from her....

MARSHA HUNT, b.1946, FROM *"REAL LIFE"*

In our relationship, Sophia is the mother and I am the daughter. She phones me regularly to keep tabs on me. When I'm not tranquil, she will try to steady me. My periods of loneliness, she reassures me. What a marvellous daughter she is! Such humanity. She has a sweetness I don't have. An understanding heart I don't have. A tranquillity.... Everything that I dreamed of for myself has happened to Sophia. I live in her image.

ROMILDA VILLANI,
FROM *"SOPHIA: LIVING AND LOVING"*

Where did she go, the small, fat creature
Staggering toward me?
Where did she go,
the shy child clutching my hand?
I feel her bird bones still,
still her face tight shut against the rain.

One day I found her gone,
a stranger in her place,
speaking another language.

Strange that I have no recollection of her return.
Yet here she is – girl grown to woman.
And having won a heart, a brain, the courage of a lion.
All the lost days brought back in friendship.

Now we meet as equals,
having forgiven one another,
having learned to love, having rediscovered laughter.

PAM BROWN, b.1928

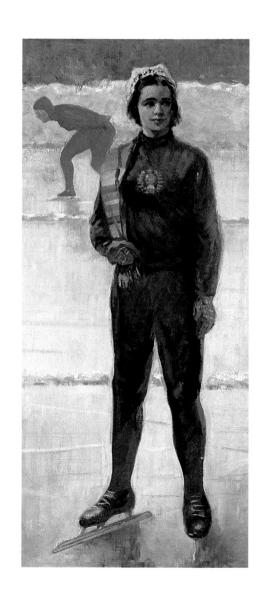

Thank you for giving me back Pooh Bear
and Ratty and Curdie and Milly-Molly-Mandy.
Thank you for reminding me
of stars and fallen leaves, winter beaches,
summer woods. Thank you for tadpoles and slow
worms and spiders named Alfred.

PAM BROWN, b.1928

The danger, as children get older, is that you will find something too intimate for comfort [in their pockets]....

"Darling," you might say, catching sight of this deeply tragic being, as surmised from a corner of a letter, a scrap of a note and two lines of obscure poetry (possibly her own), "darling, I just want to say that you know you can always talk to me, come to me for sympathy, tell me anything. Remember, I am the one who, above everybody, has your happiness closest to my heart."

Although clearly in a hurry, she stops and stares at you, apparently amazed. She may even take your arm in a protective manner. "Of course, Mum. I know that." She stares at you even more intently and sympathetically. "And remember, that I understand the difficult changes you are going through and how you have to fight depression, knowing your children are growing away from you. If you want to talk to me about anything, anything at all, please don't hesitate..."

If you have any sense, this is where the conversation ends.

RACHEL BILLINGTON, FROM *"THE FAMILY YEAR"*

Octavia was an extraordinarily beautiful child. Everyone said so, in shops and on buses and in the park, wherever we went.... I was continually amazed by the way in which I could watch for hours nothing but the small movements of her hands, and the fleeting expressions of her face. She was a very happy child, and once she learned to smile, she never stopped; at first she would smile at anything, at parking meters and dogs and strangers, but as she grew older she began to favour me, and nothing gave me more delight than her evident preference. I suppose I had not really expected her to dislike and resent me from birth, though I was quite prepared for resentment to follow later on, but I certainly had not anticipated such wreathing, dazzling gaiety of affection from her whenever I happened to catch her eye. Gradually I began to realize that she liked me, that she had no option to liking me, and that unless I took great pains to alienate her she would go on liking me, for a couple of years at least. It was very pleasant to receive such uncritical love, because it left me free to bestow love; my kisses were met by small warm rubbery unrejecting cheeks and soft dovey mumblings of delight.

MARGARET DRABBLE, b.1939, FROM *THE MILLSTONE*

You are born a woman
for the sheer glory of it,
little redhead, beautiful screamer.
You are no second sex,
but the first of the first;
& when the moon's phases
fill out the cycle
of your life,
you will crow
for the joy
of being a woman,
telling the pallid moon
to go drown herself
in the blue ocean,
& glorying, glorying, glorying
in the rosy wonder
of your sunshining wondrous self.

ERICA JONG, b.1942,
EXTRACT FROM *"ON THE FIRST NIGHT"*

What I would most like to give my daughter is freedom. And this is something that must be given by example, not by exhortation. Freedom is a loose leash, a licence to be different from your mother and still be loved.... Freedom also means letting your daughter reject you when she needs to and come back when she needs to. Freedom is unconditional love.

"Molly, I want to release you. If you hate me or want to reject me, I understand. If you curse me, then want to atone, I also understand. I expect to be your home plate: kicked, scuffed, but always returned to. I expect to be the earth from which you spring.

But if I release you too much, what will you have to fight against?

You need my acceptance, but you may need my resistance more. I promise to stand firm while you come and go. I promise unwavering love while you experiment with hate. Hate is energy too – sometimes brighter-burning energy than love. Hate is often the precondition for freedom....

I want to release you from the fears that bound me, yet I know you can only release yourself. I stand here wearing my catcher's padding. I pray you won't need me to catch you if you fall. But I'm here waiting anyway.

Freedom is full of fear. But fear isn't the worst thing we face. Paralysis is.

Letting go, I love you. Letting go, I hold you in my arms."

ERICA JONG, b.1942, FROM "FEAR OF FIFTY"

Love me always and forever, my existence depends on it... as I told you the other day you are all my joy and all my sorrow. What remains of my life is overshadowed by grief when I consider how much of it will be spent far from you.

MADAME DE SEVIGNE (1626-1696),
IN A LETTER TO HER DAUGHTER

You never <u>will</u> finish being a daughter.... You will be one when you're ninety and so will I.

GAIL GODWIN

We dads diminish in size as we grow older — but not our love.

PETER GRAY

I even love her bones.
We are so close.
She is my very best friend.

FAITH BROWN

Over the years as they and I have

pursued our own paths we have found ourselves

separated by great distances with letters forming the contact lines;

we have written to each other of our plans,

problems, hopes, achievements, disappointments and successes,

as well as our day to day happenings.

Our letters have been a strong life-line stretched half way round

the world: to me they are a continuous message of love

and dependence....

IVY SPENDER, MILTON HOSPITAL, JANUARY 1983,
FROM *"SCRIBBLING SISTERS"* BY DALE AND LYNNE SPENDER

Your first swan. Your first day by
the sea. Your first walk through a
field of spring flowers. The first time
you heard and loved Chopin. In
sharing your childhood discoveries,
I have relived my own.

MARION C. GARRETTY, b.1917

The most creative and meaningful accomplishment in my life is to have this daughter who loves, understands and respects me and gives my life real meaning. Yet, my wish for her is as old fashioned as can be; health, happiness, peace, love and a daughter for her as wonderful as she has been for me.

LYNN WILSON SPOHRER,
FROM *"A PORTRAIT OF AMERICAN MOTHERS AND DAUGHTERS"*

My dream for Ashley and Alexandra is to raise them to be all they can be, to nurture them into responsible, loving, secure, giving, human beings who not only find, but aren't afraid to go after, whatever it is that makes them happy in life.

VANESSA BELL CALLOWAY

You are our bright star.
You light our lives.
I wish you discoveries and marvels.
I wish you success that has no sting. I wish you joy and peace and warm contentment.
And always, always, love.

PAM BROWN, b.1928

I hope you find joy in the great things of life – but also in the little things.
A flower, a song, a butterfly on your hand.

ELLEN LEVINE

Thank you for
showing me, when
I thought my
mothering days were
over, that the best
days between us are
only just beginning.

PAM BROWN, b.1928

PICTURE CREDITS

Cover: © 1997 William Glackens, *The Swing*, Rosenthal.

Inlay: Peder Severin Kroyer, *A Little Girl on Skagen Beach at Sunset*, Fine Art Photographic Library.

Title-page: William Kay Blacklock, *Girl With a Thistle*, Roy Miles Gallery, London, The Bridgeman Art Library.

page 6: © 1997 Linda Benson, Artworks.

page 9: Mary Cassatt, *Children on the Beach*, National Gallery of Washington, AISA.

page 10: © 1997 Martha Walter, *Red-haired Child*, Superstock.

page 12: Carl Larsson, *Pontus*, Statens Konstmuseer.

page 15: Mary Cassatt, *Maternal Caress*, National Gallery of Art, Washington D.C., Superstock.

pages 16/17: Carl Larsson, *Garden och brygghuset*, Statens Konstmuseer.

page 18: © 1997 Diego Rivera, *Mother and Child*, Christie's Images, New York/Superstock.

page 21: Mary Cassatt, *Girl in a Garden*, Museé d'Orsay, Scala.

page 22: © 1997 Peter Vilhelm Ilsted, *A Girl Reading by a Window*, Sotheby's Transparency Library.

page 24: Albert Gustaf Edelfelt, *Luxembourg Gardens, Paris*, AISA.

page 27: Carl Larsson, *Vid kallaren*, Satens Konstmuseer.

page 29: Sir Luke Fildes, *The Doctor*, Tate Gallery, London, Art Resource.

page 31: Paul Bachem, Artworks.

page 32: F. Casana Torres, *Child at the Piano*, AISA.

page 35: Emil Orlik, *Chinese Girl*, Christie's Colour Library.

page 37: G. Pesre, *Temptation*, Private Collection, Edimedia.

page 38: R.R. Brackman, New British Museum of Art, Edimedia.

page 40: Charles Brocky, *Girl Reading at a Window*, Victoria & Albert Musuem, The Bridgeman Art Library.

page 42: Pierre Auguste Renoir, *Little Girl*, Edimedia.

page 45: Ilja Repin, *Portrait of a Girl*, Tret'jakov Gallery, Moscow, Scala.

page 47: James Fullerton Sloane, *Dressing Up*, The Bridgeman Art Library.

page 49: Gebhard Bondzin, *Annemarie*, Archiv für Kunst.

page 50: Cyprien-Eugene Boulet, *A Woman Resting Against a Tree*, Sotheby's Transparency Library.

page 53: Leonard Skeats, *Young Girl in a Mauve Hat*, The Bridgeman Art Library.

page 55: Antonio Mahilum, *Mag-Sasampaguita*, Philippine Collection.

page 56: John Dalzell Kenworthy, *Portrait of a Girl*, Private Collection, The Bridgeman Art Library.

page 58: William H. Johnson, *Lil Sis*, National Museum of American Art, Smithsonian, Art Resource.

page 61: Victor Michailowitsch Wasnezow, *Aljonuschka*, Archiv für Kunst.

page 62: Dora Hitz, *Girl in a Poppyfield*, Archiv für Kunst.

page 65: Frank Holl, *By the Fireside*, Christopher Wood Gallery, The Bridgeman Art Library.

pages 66/67: D'Espagnat, *Young Women*, Private Collection, Edimedia.

page 69: © 1997 Yaroslav Titov, *The Skater*, Bonhams, London, The Bridgeman Art Library.

page 71: Frans Wiesenthal, *The Straw Hat*, Whitford and Hughes, London, The Bridgeman Art Library.

page 72: Theo van Rysselberghe, *Garden Flowers*, Christie's, London, The Bridgeman Art Library.

page 74: © 1997 Amedeo Bocchi, *Nel prato*, Scala.

page 77: © 1997 Warren Smith, Allied Artists.

page 78: © 1997 Carlos V. Francisco, *A Girl Playing Guitar*, Collection Majent Managment and Development Corporation, Philippine Collection.

page 81: Alfred Stevens, *The Parting Letter*, Giraudon/Art Resource.

page 82: Albert Gustaf Edelfelt, *Meeting Outside the Church*, Galeria del Ateneum, Helsinki, Finland, AISA.

page 85: Henry Lerolle, *The Letter*, Musée des Beaux-Arts, The Bridgeman Art Library.

page 87: Sir Frederick William Burton, *Dreams* Fine Art Photographic Library.

page 89: © 1997 Victorio C. Edades, *Country Girl*, Collection Mr & Mrs Felipe Y Liao, Philippine Collection.

pages 90/91: Dame Laura Knight, *Summertime, Cornwall*, The Fine Art Society, London, Curtis Brown, The Bridgeman Art Library.

TEXT CREDITS

The publishers are grateful for permission to reproduce copyright material. Whilst every effort has been made to trace copyright holders, the publishers would be pleased to hear from any not here acknowledged.

ALAN BECK: Extract from *What is A Girl?* published by New England Life Insurance Co.

RACHEL BILLINGTON: Extract from *The Great Umbilical* by Rachel Billington published by Hutchinson. Extract from *The Family Year* by Rachel Billington published by Macmillan 1992, © 1992 Rachel Billington.

RICHMAL CROMPTON: Extract from *Just William.*

MARGARET DRABBLE: Extract from *The Millstone* published by Weidenfeld & Nicolson © 1968. Reprinted with permission of The Orion Publishing Group Ltd & Intercontinental Literary Agency.

DELIA EPHRON: Extract from *How to eat like a Child* published by Viking Penguin, © 1977, 1978 Delia Ephron.

VANESSA FELTZ: Extract from *'I'd like my girls blissfully married, living next door'*, article in SHE magazine, March 1997.

ART FRANK: Extract from the San Francisco Chronicle, May 1987. © Art Frank.

MICHELE GUINNESS: Extracts from *Tapestry of Voices* published by Triangle/ SPCK 1993. © 1993 Michele Guinness.

ERICA JONG: Extracts from *Fear of Fifty* by Erica Jong published by Vintage, © Erica Mann Jong 1994. Extract from *'On the First Night'* from Ordinary Miracles, published by Plume. Copyright Erica Jong 1983.

GROUCHO MARX: Extracts from *Love, Groucho* published by Faber and Faber, © 1992 Miriam Marx Allen.

MARGARET MEAD: Extract from *Blackberry Winter* published by Angus and Robertson, an imprint of HarperCollins Publishers Ltd.

HELEN THOMAS: Extract from *Under Storm's Wing,* published by Paladin/Grafton, © 1988 Myfanwy Thomas.